FACTS AT YOUR FINGERTIPS

EARTH

DAVID MARSHALL

SIMON & SCHUSTER
YOUNG BOOKS

Commissioning editor: Daphne Butler
Design and artwork: SPL Design
Photographs: ZEFA, except for
Aerofilms 25
NHPA 9, 20t
Robert Harding 10t, 20b, 27
Typesetting and layout: Quark Xpress

First published in Great Britain in 1992
by Simon & Schuster Young Books

Simon & Schuster Young Books
Campus 400, Maylands Avenue
Hemel Hempstead, Herts HP2 7EZ

Printed and bound in Belgium
by Proost International Book Production

A catalogue record for this book
is available from the British Library
ISBN 0 7500 1084 3

CONTENTS

WHAT IS THE

EARTH ?

The Earth is one of the nine planets that orbit the sun. It has air all around it, and just the right mixture of sun and rain for life to prosper. It is also the perfect distance from the sun to be neither too hot nor too cold. ➤

◄ Because most humans live on land, they don't realise that about three-quarters of the Earth's surface is covered by oceans and seas. The largest ocean is the Pacific Ocean and that covers about a third of the Earth's surface on its own.

Some of the Earth is too dry, too cold, too mountainous or too densely forested for many animals to live successfully. But parts of the Earth are just right for life, and the Earth can support a wonderful variety of plants and animals. ➤

HOW THE EARTH BEGAN

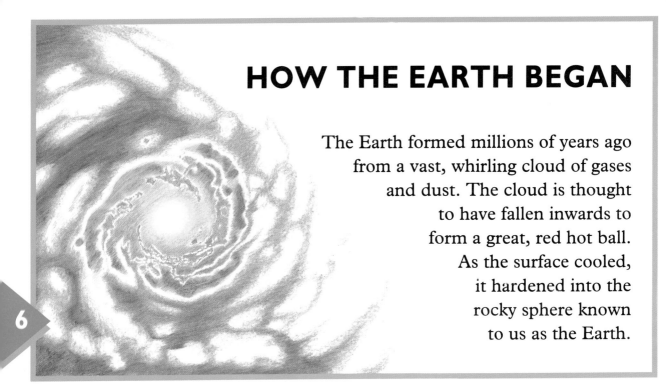

The Earth formed millions of years ago from a vast, whirling cloud of gases and dust. The cloud is thought to have fallen inwards to form a great, red hot ball. As the surface cooled, it hardened into the rocky sphere known to us as the Earth.

LAND AND WATER

Because at first the Earth was very hot, steam rose from the surface and formed clouds which gradually cooled as the air around them cooled.

The steam which had formed the clouds condensed into water droplets and rain fell for many years creating oceans and seas on the Earth, as the water collected wherever the surface was uneven.

WHAT IT'S LIKE INSIDE

The hard thin surface of the Earth is called the crust. Underneath, there is a thick layer known as the mantle, and at the very centre of the Earth is the core. The core is mostly made of iron with some nickel and is the source of the Earth's magnetic field.

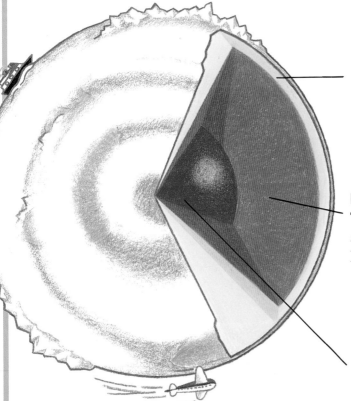

CRUST
Under the oceans the crust may be as little as 6 km thick, whereas under the land it may be as much as 40 km thick.

MANTLE
This is about 2,900 km thick and comprises over half the Earth's mass.

CORE
The core has a radius of 3,470 km and comprises about a third of the Earth's mass.

The mantle is made of hot heavy rocks which in parts are like molten treacle. The crust can slide on this toffee-like layer and where two pieces of crust (called plates) meet, they push up mountains and cause volcanoes and earthquakes.

DIFFERENT ROCKS

There are many different kinds of rock on Earth which all fall into three basic types: igneous, sedimentary and metamorphic.

▲ Granite

IGNEOUS ROCK
Forms when volcanic lava cools and hardens. Lava solidifying under the ground becomes granite, runny lava basalt, and gassy lava pumice.

▲ Limestone

SEDIMENTARY ROCK
Forms when stones, mud and sand (sediment) settle in layers on the seabed, and harden into rock over thousands of years.

▲ Marble

METAMORPHIC ROCK
Forms deep in the Earth from existing sedimentary rock, changed by extreme heat and pressure. Marble exists in various colours.

▲ Basalt is a dense igneous rock which forms in columns.

EROSION

Rocks are constantly being worn away by the weather. High temperatures, ice and snow, running water and wind all wear away the rocks, breaking off bits and sweeping them away. Rocks in desert areas are often worn into weird and wonderful shapes. Rivers carry the silt and debris of the land down to the seas.

THE EQUATOR

The equator is an imaginary line round the middle of the Earth where the sun is always directly overhead at midday and it is always hot. It often rains every day and plants and trees grow very quickly.

◄The rainforest in Brazil is the largest forest in the world.

THE POLES

The poles are imaginary points at the very far north and very far south of the Earth. They are the furthest points from the equator and the coldest places on Earth. In mid-winter they have constant night, and in mid-summer constant daylight. We call the area around the north pole the Arctic and around the south pole the Antarctic.

Polar bears have thick fur coats to keep them warm in the icy Arctic Ocean.►

LATITUDE

Lines of latitude are imaginary
lines round the Earth at
standard intervals from
the equator. They are
measured in degrees
with the equator being
0° and the poles 90°.
Times Square in New York
is on a latitude just over 40°N
of the equator.

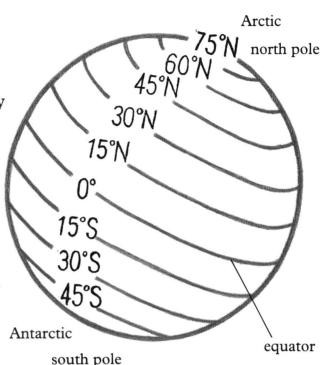

Arctic
75°N   north pole
60°N
45°N
30°N
15°N
0°
15°S
30°S
45°S

Antarctic
south pole
equator

LONGITUDE

north pole

Prime Meridian

60°W
45°W 30°W
15°W 0° 15°E 45°E
30°E

Lines of longitude are imaginary
lines drawn round the Earth at
right angles to the equator.
Like latitude, they are
measured in degrees.
The Prime Meridian is
0° and it runs through
Greenwich in England.
From Greenwich lines go
east and west until they meet at
180° on the other side of the Earth.

south pole

MOVING CONTINENTS

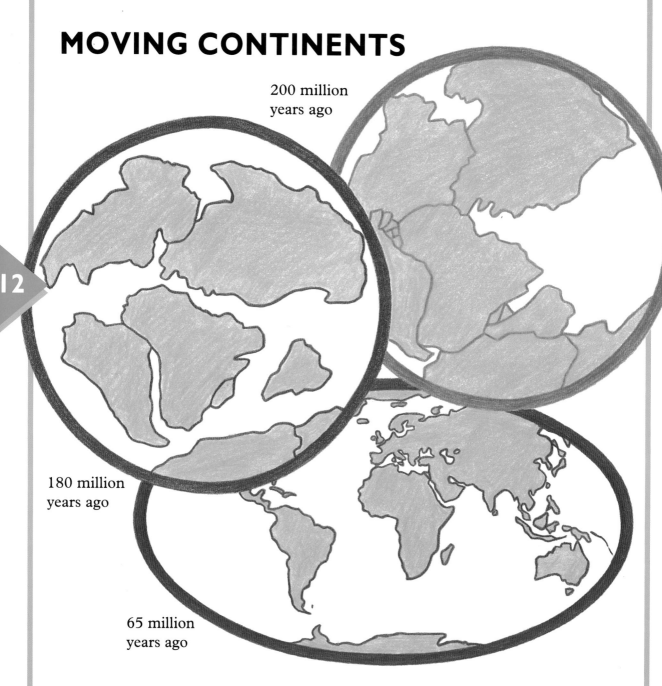

200 million
years ago

180 million
years ago

65 million
years ago

The land began as one big continent called Pangaea 200 million years ago. This slowly broke into pieces that drifted apart to the seven continents we know today.

The scientist Alfred Wegener first realised about the idea of 'continental drift'. The continents are all still moving and the Atlantic Ocean becomes 2-4 cm wider each year.

VOLCANOES AND EARTHQUAKES

At some points in the Earth's crust, pressures and heat make the rocks turn to magma. Magma is very hot and thick like treacle. It forces its way to the surface and explodes out as a volcano. Some volcanoes have very runny lava, others throw up rocks, ash and gas. There are about 450 active volcanoes on Earth.

Earthquakes are caused by sudden movement of the rocks. Every year there are over 5000 earthquakes. Some are small but some are so violent that whole towns and villages are destroyed.

▲ Volcanic eruption on Hawaii in the Pacific Ocean. Runny lava is thrown high into the air

PLATES

The Earth's crust is rather like an egg shell cracked into 15 pieces called plates. Where the edges of plates meet, one plate often slides under the other pushing it up into mountains. There are stresses in the rocks under some mountains which cause volcanoes.

volcanoes erupt because of stresses in the rocks

new crust forming under the ocean

two plates meet—one slides down and the other pushes up

crust

LIFE ON

EARTH

Animals and plants probably appeared in the seas and oceans about 700 million years ago. These simple life forms gradually evolved, producing the millions of creatures on Earth today. ►

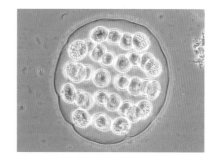

◄ Many creatures died out and became extinct. Huge reptiles called dinosaurs, which dominated the Earth for about 120 million years, suddenly disappeared about 65 million years ago, and mammals gradually took over.

There were also human-like creatures that became extinct. There are paintings in caves in southern Europe showing the life of Cro-Magnon people who lived there 35,000 years ago. ►

PLANTS

Plants grow wherever they can on Earth. Near the equator in South America and western Africa, there are huge forests where the temperature never drops below 17°C. It rains every day and these forests are teeming with life. As you move further away from the equator, the temperature drops steadily, there is less rain and the sun is weaker. It is more difficult for plants to grow but they adapt so that they can live through drought and freezing winters.

Plants grow by making their own food by taking carbon dioxide from the air and water from the ground. They convert these into food by using sunlight and the green substance in their leaves called chlorophyll. We call this process photosynthesis.

Sunlight on fresh new leaves in a forest in Europe. Each year deciduous trees grow new leaves. ➤

FLOWERS AND FRUITS

PETALS
Brightly coloured to attract insects.

CARPEL
The part of the flower that turns into the fruit and seed case.

LEAVES
Contain chlorophyll which makes food from carbon dioxide and water in sunlight.

SOIL
Contains minerals which dissolve in water to feed plants.

ROOTS
Hold the plant firm in the soil and take in water.

FLOWERS
Many plants produce flowers which later turn to fruit. The fruit contains seeds to make new plants.

FRUITS
Fruits come in all shapes and sizes. Many of them are specially grown by people as food. These fruits grow only in tropical countries. They are coconut, pineapple, banana, mango and durian.

MAMMALS

Mammals are warm-blooded animals that usually have a hairy skin. There are many different kinds and sizes—from bats and shrews that weigh a few grammes, to the blue whale that weighs over a 100 tonnes and is the largest mammal that has ever existed.

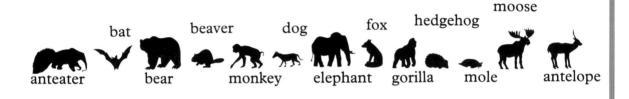

anteater • bat • bear • beaver • monkey • dog • elephant • fox • gorilla • hedgehog • mole • moose • antelope

impala • gerenuk • onyx

▲ Some of the mammals that live on Earth. Altogether there are 19 different orders of mammals, and 4,060 living species.

Mammals live all over the world. Some can live on the ice caps, others in deserts and others in the oceans, but most live on land where it is fairly warm and there is plenty of food to eat and fresh water to drink.

◄ Baby mammals, like these lambs, start their lives inside their mother's bodies. After they are born they feed on milk from glands—called mammary glands—on her body until they are mature enough to eat adult food.

HUMANKIND

Humans developed over thousands of years from the same ancestor as apes and monkeys.

By chance humans grew large brains and nimble fingers. This enabled them to use the materials in their environment to make tools and to feed, clothe and house themselves. They discovered fire to keep themselves warm and cook their food. At the same time, they developed language which meant they could talk to each other and pass on information.

It took thousands of years for the world's population to grow. By 1830, it had reached about one thousand million. By 1975 it reached four thousand million and by 1987, five thousand million—and it's still growing.

19

MARSUPIALS

Marsupials are a special group of mammals. There are about 250 species. Newborn babies attach themselves to their mother's milk glands and stay there until they finish growing. Usually the glands are inside a pouch in which the baby lives for many months. Most marsupials are native to Australia and include kangaroos, wallabies, koalas and bandicoots.

An Australian red-necked wallaby with a baby in its pouch. ►

REPTILES AND AMPHIBIANS

▲ Iguanas are a large lizards that live mostly in South America. Their skins have strange scales.

Reptiles are cold-blooded animals which have scaly skins and lay eggs with hard shells. There are about 6,000 species. Amphibians are like reptiles but live partly on land and partly in water. The young are born in water from eggs with no shells and go through a change, called metamorphosis, before becoming adult. There are about 2,400 species.

INSECTS

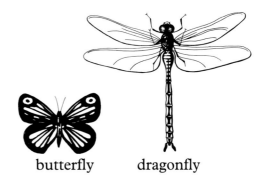

ant   earwig   fly   beetle   butterfly   dragonfly

Insects have six legs, and bodies that have three parts—a head, a thorax and an abdomen. Some, but not all, have wings. There are millions of different species.

Size varies from less than 1 mm to nearly 300 mm, and colours vary from dull brown and black to brilliant blues, yellows, reds and greens.

BIRDS

Birds are warm-blooded animals with feathers and wings. Nearly all birds use their wings to fly and some travel enormous distances. Each year, parent birds build nests and lay eggs. They sit on the eggs till the young hatch, and feed them until they are able to live alone.

▲Kingfisher

There are more than 8,700 different species. The tiny bee hummingbird is only 6 cm long. The albatross's wings span over 3.5 m and the trumpeter swan can weigh as much as 17 kg.

USING THE

EARTH

Everything existing on the Earth is part of a fantastic web. Plants and animals all use the resources of the Earth but the biggest users of all are human. ►

◄ People are using up the resources of the Earth and as the population grows, more and more land is taken over for their needs leaving less for other animals.

People enjoy the beauty of the Earth, but their activities can damage the very thing they enjoy. We need to take care of our environment. ►

HOMES

Homes are very special places where we can eat, sleep and keep our possessions. They are safe places where our families can relax and will be warm and dry in bad weather. People build homes wherever they live. Some homes are isolated but very many are clustered together in towns and cities.

FACTORIES

In the 17th century people started to move to the cities to work in the new factories. Many people were needed to operate the new steam-powered machines. Nowadays, goods are often made by robots and only a few people control the machines.

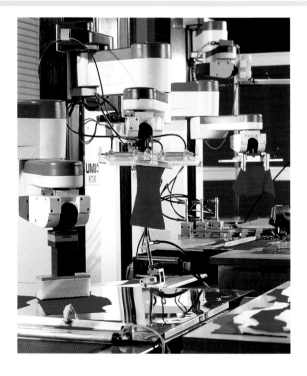

Robots do many jobs in factories where the same task is repeated over and over. This machine is sewing cloth together to make clothes. ►

ROADS AND RAILWAYS

Once there were no roads or railways, only footpaths for people travelling on foot or riding on horseback. The Romans were the first people to build good roads about 2000 years ago. Today, many countries have motorways so that cars and lorries can move quickly from place to place.

The first railway was opened in 1829 between Stockton and Darlington in northern England. Just 47 years later, there were over 400,000 km of railway track in the USA and many other countries were building rail networks.

Roads and railways sometimes now run side by side, the newer motorways spanning the ageing tracks. ►

FARMING

◄ Nearly all of the food we eat has been grown somewhere on a farm. Farms grow the crops suited to the climate and the soil in their area. The two most important crops worldwide are wheat and rice.

Farms also keep cattle, sheep, pigs, chickens and various other animals. Most animals are sold for meat, but cattle are also kept for milk, sheep for wool and chickens for eggs. ►

◄ Modern machinery means that farms are more efficient but also that they need fewer workers. Hedgerows and walls have given way to larger fields and wildlife has disappeared along with their habitat.

The first humans soon learnt that keeping animals and growing crops was easier than hunting and gathering food. For thousands of years until the Industrial Revolution 90 per cent of the population worked on farms. Even today more than half the 5 thousand million people on this planet are engaged in farming.

MINING

Mining is one of the oldest human activities. Archaeologists in South Africa have found evidence that an iron mine was worked there 43,000 years ago. Certainly the Egyptians mined copper and turquoise about 3400 BC. Today, we take many minerals from the ground. Iron and other metals, coal and oil, and gem stones like diamonds are all very important to our industry. To extract and use these resources we need vast amounts of energy. Coal, oil and nuclear fuel are used in power stations to make electricity. But they all produce poisonous waste and once we have used them they cannot be replaced.

Steel is made from molten iron. Huge amounts of energy are needed to melt the iron ore. ►

SPOILING THE EARTH

People have only recently realised the damage they are causing to the Earth. The fumes from cars and industry are making the rain acid destroying plant life. Cutting down trees in the rainforests is upsetting the natural balance of oxygen and carbon dioxide in the air. Careless farming methods are wasting the soil and helping to create deserts.

▲ A tree killed by acid rain.

▼ Old tyres don't rot away!

So many of the Earth's resources are used to make things that are then thrown away. They don't rot down like waste vegetable matter. They just lie on the land making it useless. Other waste products are so poisonous they must be sealed in special tanks and hidden under the Earth.

WHAT KIND OF FUTURE?

Our Earth needs protection to ensure there is a healthy future for all its species. People must think up ways to use its resources sensibly and not waste them. If we learn once more to reuse and recycle things rather than throw them away, we will make the most of what we have. We must exploit our forests with great care. They protect the soil from erosion and provide vital oxygen to the atmosphere. They also provide fuel, pulp to make paper and timber to build with.

If people adapt their ways of farming they will gain the maximum food from the land for the least damage to it.

◄ Fields of mustard seed in Canada make a beautiful picture, but do we always farm the land in the best way?

FACTS ABOUT EARTH

Caspian Sea, largest lake but really an inland sea, 371,800 square kilometres.

Longest glacier is the Lambert-Fisher ice passage—515 km.

Deepest ocean, Marianas Trench, more than 10,900 metres deep.

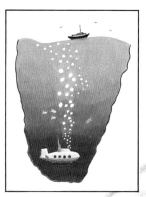

Total area of Earth's surface is 510 million square kilometres

Highest temperature ever recorded, Libya in 1922, 58°C in the shade.

Longest river is the Nile—6670 km.

Highest
point,
Mt Everest,
8.848 km.

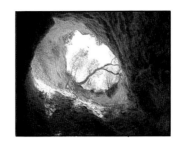

Deepest cave is over
1494 metres deep in
the French Alps.

Highest rainfall
ever recorded
in 24 hours is
1870 mm on the
island of Reunion.

Lowest
temperature
ever recorded,
−89.2°C
in Russia.

Most poisonous
land snakes
—fierce snake
and tiger snake—
live in Australia.

INDEX